Having departed Moana, west of the Southern Alps, and now running beside the Arnold River, the TranzAlpine, led by locomotive Dx 5212, is on the last leg of the journey from Christchurch to Greymouth. The snow-capped peak is Mount Alexander, 1958 metres.

D1408545

The TranzAlpine, or simply the 'Tranz', is New Zealand's well-kn[illegible] [illegible]rist train that each morning [illegible] kilometre journey to Grey[illegible] - millimetre) single track c[illegible] y Plains, twists and turns above de[illegible] h spindly viaducts, passes through 19 tunnels (one [illegible]-metres long) and continues on beside rain forests, past lakes said to be teeming with trout, and through more tunnels, until it reaches its destination a short distance from the waves crashing off the Tasman Sea.

Stately Christchurch (population 350,000), on the South Island's east (Pacific) coast is arguably the most 'English' of cities outside England. Greymouth (population about 8000) is a town built around a one-time busy port on the Grey River. Still bearing the hallmarks of a boom or bust town, Greymouth is precariously bounded by mountains, the river and the Tasman Sea.

The TranzAlpine, with some justification, claims to be one of the world's great rail journeys. With an onboard licensed buffet and often quirky commentaries provided by train managers, the Tranz carries more tourist travellers than local people. The one train makes a return journey to Greymouth (each way is less than five hours) making it ideally suited for a day excursion from Christchurch. The Tranz can also be used as the start of a journey into Westland - the West Coast - with its Shantytown museum, coal and gold mines, jade rivers and magnificent national parks boasting scenery endowed with World Heritage status.

As the train reaches Springfield on the first leg of the journey, TranzAlpine passengers will hear about the border collie, Rosie who not so long ago met the train each day and was rewarded with a pre-heated railway meat pie. When she died in April 1996, and went to the big pie in th sky, Rosie was thought to have consumed more than 5000 pies since the TranzAlpine started in 1987. Rosie was aged 21 when she was photographed with her master, former Springfield railway employee, Keith Williams.

East of the Southern Alps the TranzAlpine climbs the Avoca bank a short distance beyond tunnel No. 16 and Slovens Creek, the last of the high viaducts. Winter frost transforms an otherwise brown landscape of tussock and mountain scree.

Down at the Station

The TranzAlpine journey starts at Christchurch's stylish railway terminal opened in 1993 on a site previously occupied by the New Zealand Railways' Addington railway workshops. Contrasting with the modern styling and extensive use of glass are a number of remnants from the past.

The Passchendaele plaque, was for many years mounted on a well-loved steam locomotive, Ab 608, to commemorate the New Zealand railwaymen's involvement in the First World War.

A not uncommon visitor to the rail terminal is W 192, the first locomotive built at the Addington railway workshops in 1889. W 192, a 2-6-2T, is also the first New Zealand Railways'-built locomotive. It is preserved as part of the Railway Heritage Trust of New Zealand.

The 21.9-metre concrete tower, was constructed in 1883 to supply high-pressure water to the railway workshops. Built by prison labour, it is believed to be one of the world's first reinforced concrete structures. A keen eye may detect the tower's slight lean.

The TranzAlpine journey starts in earnest at Springfield, reached an hour after departing Christchurch. Here the Tranz faces its first alpine barrier, the Torlesse Range (1981 metres). Springfield was once a staging post on the railway where Kb class 4-8-4 steam locomotives were stabled, ready to haul trains on the 140-kilometre mountain run through to Arthur's Pass.

The Waimakariri Gorge seen from the 72-metre-high Staircase viaduct, the highest on the trans-alpine route. Waimakariri is Maori for 'cold rushing water' and is known for its aqua-blue colour. Here, east of the Southern Alps, rivers run towards the Pacific Ocean.

Unseen by TranzAlpine passengers, but nevertheless close to the railway at Springfield, is a monument to Rewi Alley, a Springfield-born New Zealander who spent most of his life in China, where he set up industrial co-operatives during the 1930s. His father, a Springfield school teacher, refused to teach the young Rewi, who had to walk more than 7 kilometres to another school.

TranzAlpine passengers enjoy spectacular views of the Waimakariri Gorge, a few kilometres beyond Springfield. On this section the TranzAlpine passes through 16 of the 19 tunnels on the railway, and crosses five high viaducts.

During its first year in service, in 1988, the TranzAlpine won a New Zealand Tourism Award in the Tours Section. These photographs show the train running at that time. Being hauled by Mitsubishi-built Dj class locomotives, (above), descending the Cass Bank, surrounded by tussock valleys and mountains of greywacke, a hard sandstone, and (below), it is crossing the 55-metre-high Broken River viaduct in limestone country.

A more recent view of the TranzAlpine, hauled by locomotive Dx 5391, approaching Cass, a tiny settlement 24 kilometres from Arthur's Pass.

Lake Sarah, named by Joe Pearson after his wife, is one of a number of popular trout fishing lakes in the upper Waimakariri basin. Pearson named a nearby larger lake after himself.

The alpine-style Arthur

Kea, or mountain parrots, may be seen lurking around the station. If given the chance, these comical exhibitionists will play a prank on unsuspecting train passengers. Hold tightly to those treasured brightly

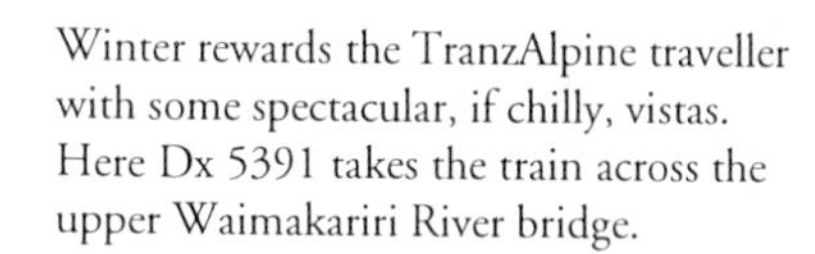

Winter rewards the TranzAlpine traveller with some spectacular, if chilly, vistas. Here Dx 5391 takes the train across the upper Waimakariri River bridge.

Everything is frozen on a frosty winter morning, even the branches of willow trees lining the Waimakariri River.

Winter steam excursio
thundering up to Arth
Pass recall a glamorous
of the past. Here, a 4-
Ka 942, has just arrive
with a packed train fr
Christchurch. Ka 942
privately owned by
Wellington businessm
Ian Welch, was built i
New Zealand in 1940

The 150-metre-high Devil's Punchbowl Falls are the most impressive of the Arthur's Pass National Park waterfalls. They are reached after a 40-minute walk through mountain beech forest from the Arthur's Pass township.

The TranzAlpine departs Arthur's Pass and crosses the Bealey River before entering the 8.5-kilometre Otira Tunnel beneath the Southern Alps. By this stage of the journey - less than three hours from Christchurch - the train has passed through many diverse landscapes. The tunnel divides more landscapes, and even climates; it could be raining at the other end.

Beneath the 1823m snow summit of Mount Bealey, a pair of DFT locomotives, No. 7092 and No. 7254, lift a 12-total TranzAlpine, loaded with 420 passengers, away from the Arthur's Pass stop

5391

7092
7092
7092
DFT7092
Tranz Rail

The tiny railway station of Ruru is all that remains of a once thriving sawmill settlement. Built around 1894, the station has been preserved by the Rail Heritage Trust.

The TranzApline has become a popular journey for overseas visitors.

A locomotive driver's view of the track ahead as it runs beside the Taramakau River between Aickens and Jacksons, west of the Southern Alps. This is Westland, better known as the West Coast, where the rivers run towards the Tasman Sea.

Jacksons Pub, supposedly famous for possum pies, recalls pre-railway days when coaching inns stood at intervals along the trans-alpine route. Such establishments were welcome sites for coach drivers, weary passengers and, of course, the horse teams. The pub is a short distance above the small Jacksons wayside railway station and the Taramakau River.

Wearing the new Tranz Scenic colours introduced late 1995, the TranzAlpine headed by a pair of DFT locomotives, passes through lush Westland farmlands near Moana. Lake Brunner is glimpsed in the background. By this stage of the journey the TranzAlpine has crossed the Alpine Fault near Inchbonnie. The fault, responsible for many severe earthquakes, divides the newer eastern mountains of sedimentary limestone and greywacke rock (much of it built up during the last million years), from older West Coast landforms of granite and other metamorphic rock. These older landforms contain gold.

7254
Tranz Rail
Tranz Rail
7092

ABUROC

Close to the railway a helicopter loads sphagnum moss lifted from nearby swamps. The spongy moss is exported to Japan where it is used in orchid growing.

TranzAlpine locomotive driver Graeme Twist checks train schedule details with Train Control.

Lake Brunner, the largest lake close to the trans-alpine railway, was named to honour Thomas Brunner, the first European to explore the lake in 1848. Brunner's diaries tell of an incredible 550-day journey through West Coast forests during which, in order to survive, he had to eat his faithful dog. Popular with trout fishermen, the lake fills a large hollow carved out by former glaciers.

The TranzAlpine pauses at Kotuku to cross (pass) a unit coal train carrying export West Coast coal to Port Lyttelton near Christchurch.

The TranzAlpine skirts around an embankment above the Grey river before entering tunnel No. 19.

A short distance past Stillwater, rusting pieces of old machinery at the Brunner coal mine are poignant reminders of New Zealand's worst coal mining disaster when, in 1896, an explosion in a disused section of the mine ripped through the shafts, killing 67 people. This monument was unvieled in 1996 to mark the centenary of the disaster.

Near Greymouth the Grey River has forged a wide path through limestone hills. The rustic old railway bridge still carries coal trains from mines on the north side of the river. A TranzAlpine service, on the far side of the Grey, is almost at journey's end.

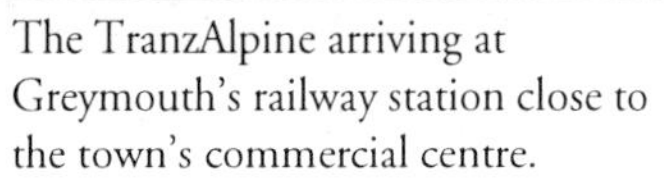
The TranzAlpine arriving at Greymouth's railway station close to the town's commercial centre.

Moments later the platform becomes a busy place as travellers hurry to board on-going transport to Westport or South Westland destinations, or to join a tour of the town.

In its heyday, Greymouth on the Grey River - named after Sir George Grey who was twice governor and once prime minister of New Zealand - was a busy river port frequented by ships plying the New Zealand coast and crossing the Tasman Sea from Australia. The port has all but vanished, leaving a number of active fishing vessels as reminders of bygone days.

Greymouth's commercial centre has frequently been flooded by the Grey River, prompting the recent building of an impressive flood wall. The river is known for its cold wind, 'the Barber', which funnels down from the inland gorge. As locals will tell you 'the wind is so sharp, it will cut your throat'.

Jade, like gold, is part of the geological, social and cultural make-up of the West Coast and its inhabitants: most families display, at the very least, a small jade treasure. The West Coast is one of the few places in the world where jade is found, and it was nephrite jade (greenstone) that brought the first trans-alpine travellers - the Maori - to the Coast early last century. To the Maori the South Island was known as Te Wahi Pounamu (the place of greenstone). Today one of the best places to see the almost magical stone is at Greymouth's Jade Boulder Gallery in Guinness Street. On display are superb pieces from New Zealand jade carvers.

Ian Boustridge (left) has earned a well-deserved reputation for his work, which is held in private collections throughout the world. Among his favourite pieces is a head sculpture in white and green jade (lower left). As with all his work, this piece demonstrates a finish achieved only by a perfectionist. Along with other carvers, he is often seen working at the gallery, which has a large display area, the Rare Discovery craft shop and the fully licensed Jade Rock Café. A special feature is a fascinating 'please touch' Discovery Walkway which shows visitors the origins and discovery of jade. If you are on a day excursion, take care not to become too engrossed or you will miss your train back to Christchurch.

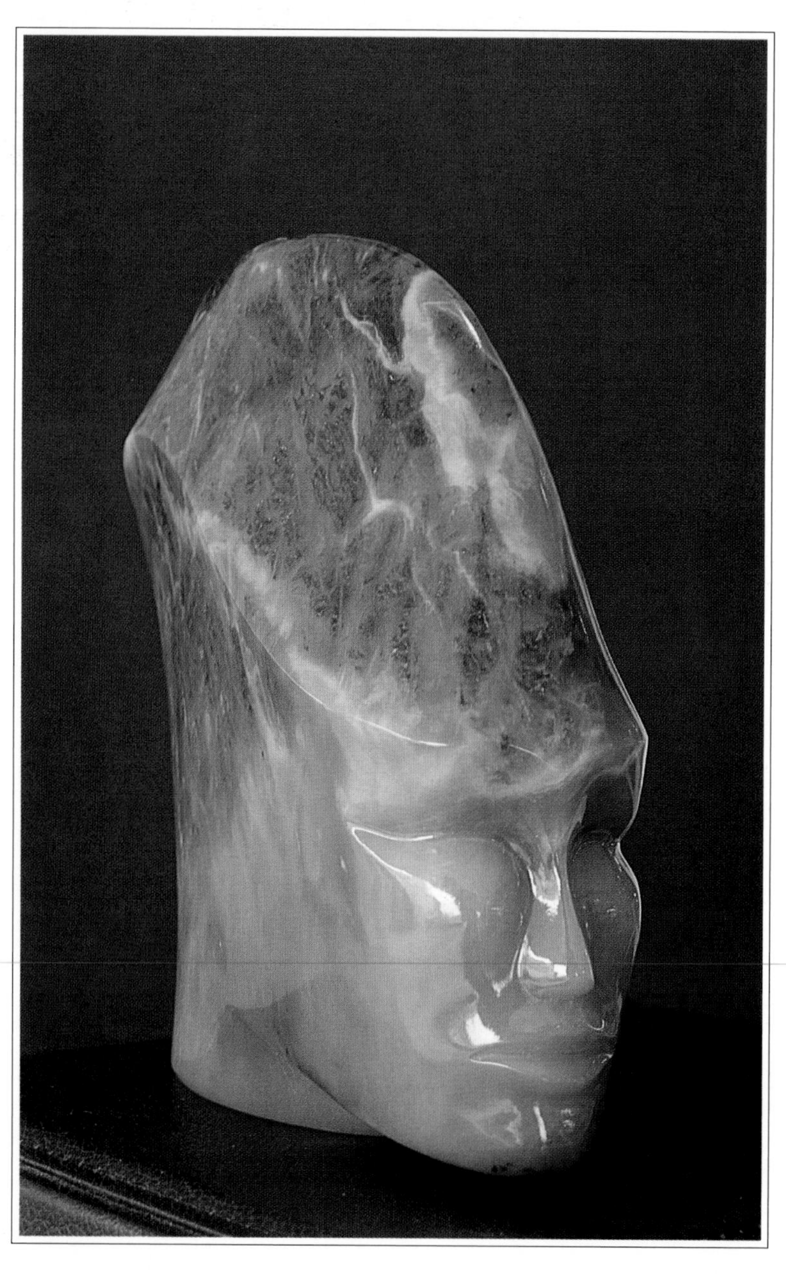

Shantytown (right) is one of the not-to-be-missed attractions for train travellers staying to explore the West Coast. Shantytown, owned and operated by the West Coast Historical and Mechanical Society, emulates a West Coast gold mining town of the turn of the century, complete with its own sluicing claim.

The little train with a big puff (above) is seen at the Shantytown museum 12 kilometres south of Greymouth. A trip on a re-created West Coast bush railway takes about 15 minutes and includes a stop at a replica sawmill. The locomotive is an Fa class 0-6-0 built in 1897 by Sharp & Stewart of Glasgow.

Visions of Westland

Left: Lake Mahinapua near Hokitika, south of Greymouth, is one of many idyllic lakes backed by native forests and high inland mountains.

Below left: The Paparoa National Park, north of Greymouth, features the Punakaiki Pancake Rocks - stratified limestone stacks - and Blowholes that are best seen at high tide during heavy weather.

Right: Archetypal West Coaster Les Lisle of the Mahinapua Hotel, is seen here serving one of his whitebait patties, a West Coast delicacy.

Below: Gina Pavanetto, from Italy, enjoys South Westland views.

Below right: Keith Detlaff, at Róss, is one of many West Coasters who will help you to pan for a few specks of gold.

Ice pinnacles on the Fox Glacier, Westland National Park.

New Zealand's two highest mountains, Mount Tasman (3496 metres), left, and Mount Cook (3754 metres), reach for the skies just a short distance from the South Westland coast. This view is near the Fox Glacier village, 217 kilometres south of Greymouth.

The remains of a once prosperous gold dredge at Gillespies Beach, South Westland.

A forgotten bush tramway rusts away in a Westland forest.

Tranz Rail
Tranz Rail
Tranz Scenic

Just a few days after Tranz Scenic rail services won the 1997 New Zealand Tourism Award (Transportation Section), the TranzAlpine, headed by DFT locomotives No. 7254 and No. 7092, was caught beside the Arnold River, near Moana, on the return journey to Christchurch. The West Coast is known for its native rain forests and ferns, supported by frequent rain storms borne on prevailing westerly winds crossing the Tasman Sea. Unlike the mountain beech forests of the east, West Coast forests have, until recently, been extensively milled. These days most New Zealand native forests are protected, including trees on private properties.

The TranzAlpine departs Greymouth for Christchurch.

A mural on a Greymouth building depicts a similar scene to the one above, as it was at the turn of the century.